CATS!
CATS!

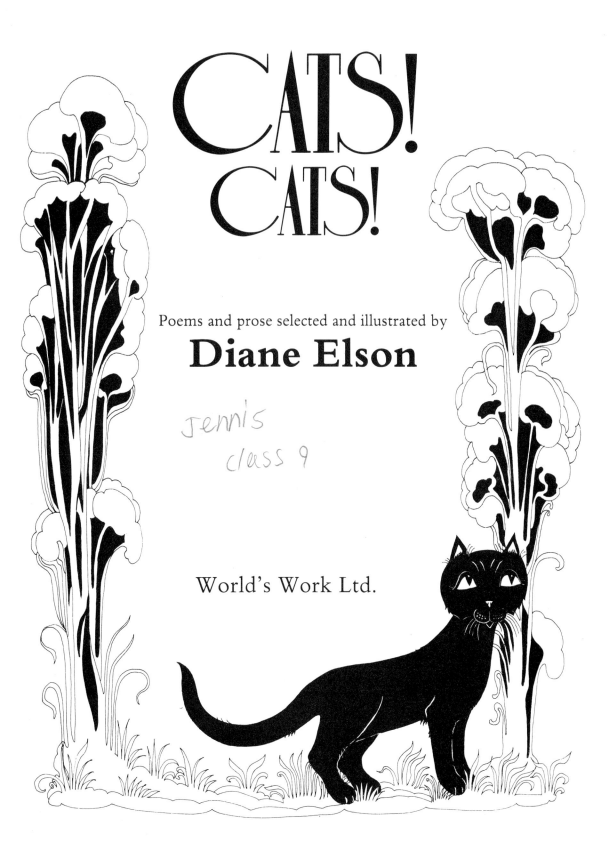

CATS! CATS!

Poems and prose selected and illustrated by

Diane Elson

Jenni's
class 9

World's Work Ltd.

Illustrations copyright 1984 by Diane Elson
Published 1984 by
World's Work Ltd.
The Windmill Press, Kingswood, Tadworth, Surrey
Printed in Great Britain by
Blantyre Printing and Binding Co. Ltd.
0 437 377067

For Hushabi and Smutty

As I was going to St. Ives

As I was going to St. Ives,
I met a man with seven wives,
Each wife had seven sacks,
Each sack had seven cats,
Each cat had seven kits:
Kits, cats, sacks, and wives,
How many were there going to St. Ives?

Answer; only one

Pussy

I like little pussy, her coat is so warm;
And if I don't hurt her, she'll do me no harm.
So I'll not pull her tail, nor drive her away,
But pussy and I very gently will play.
She shall sit by my side, and I'll give her some food;
And she'll love me because I am gentle and good.

I'll pat pretty pussy, and then she will purr;
And thus show her thanks for my kindness to her.
But I'll not pinch her ears, nor tread on her paw,
Lest I should provoke her to use her sharp claw.
I never will vex her, nor make her displeased—
For pussy don't like to be worried and teased.

Dame Trot

Dame Trot and her cat
Sat down for a chat;
The Dame sat on this side
And puss sat on that.

Puss, says the Dame,
Can you catch a rat,
Or a mouse in the dark?
Purr, says the cat.

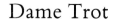

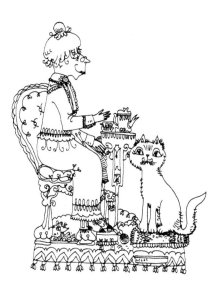

Diddlety, Diddlety, Dumpty

Diddlety, diddlety, dumpty
The cat ran up the plum tree;
Half a crown
To fetch her down
Diddlety, diddlety, dumpty.

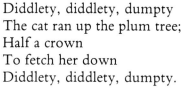

Pussicat, Wussicat

Pussicat, wussicat, with a white foot,
When is your wedding, and I'll come to it.
The beer's to brew, the bread's to bake,
Pussicat, wussicat, don't be too late.

Five little pussy cats

Five little pussy cats sitting in a row,
Blue ribbons round each neck, fastened in a bow.
Hey pussies! Ho pussies! Are your faces clean?
Don't you know you're sitting there so as to be seen.

Who's that ringing?

Who's that ringing
At my door bell?
A little pussy cat
That isn't very well.
Rub its little nose
With a little mutton fat,
For that's the best cure
For a little pussy cat.

Pussy cat sits beside the fire

Pussy cat sits beside the fire,
So pretty and so fair.
In walks the little dog,
Ah, Pussy, are you there?
How do you do, Mistress Pussy?
Mistress Pussy, how do you do?
I thank you kindly, little dog,
I'm very well just now.

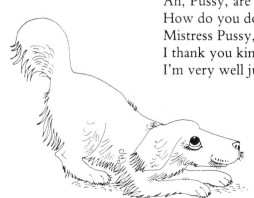

To a cat

John Keats

Cat! who hast pass'd thy grand climacteric,
How many mice and rats hast in thy days
Destroy'd?—How many titbits stolen? Gaze
With those bright languid segments green, and prick
Those velvet ears—but pr'ythee do not stick
Thy latent talons in me—and upraise
Thy gentle mew—and tell me all thy frays
Of fish and mice, and rats and tender chick.
Nay, look not down, nor lick thy dainty wrists—
For all the wheezy asthma,—and for all
Thy tail's tip is nick'd off—and though the fists
Of many a maid have given thee many a maul,
Still is that fur as soft as when the lists
In youth thou enter'dst on glass bottled wall.

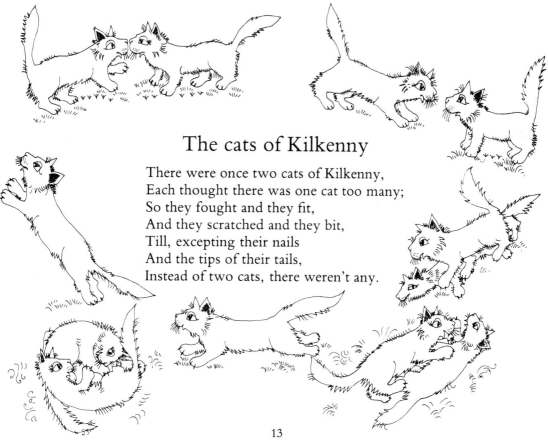

The cats of Kilkenny

There were once two cats of Kilkenny,
Each thought there was one cat too many;
So they fought and they fit,
And they scratched and they bit,
Till, excepting their nails
And the tips of their tails,
Instead of two cats, there weren't any.

Pussy cat ate the dumplings

Pussy cat ate the dumplings
Pussy cat ate the dumplings
Mamma stood by, and cried, Oh, fie!
Why did you eat the dumplings?

Hie, hie

Hie, hie, says Anthony,
Puss is in the pantry,
Gnawing, gnawing, a mutton mutton-bone;
See how she tumbles it,
See how she mumbles it,
See how she tosses the mutton mutton-bone.

The Owl and the Pussy-cat

Edward Lear

The Owl and the Pussy-cat went to sea
In a beautiful pea-green boat,
They took some honey, and plenty of money,
Wrapped up in a five-pound note.
The Owl looked up to the stars above,
And sang to a small guitar,
"O lovely Pussy! O Pussy, my love,
What a beautiful Pussy you are,
You are,
You are!
What a beautiful Pussy you are!"

Pussy said to the Owl, "You elegant fowl!
How charmingly sweet you sing!
O let us be married! too long we have tarried:
But what shall we do for a ring?"
They sailed away for a year and a day,
To the land where the Bong-tree grows,

And there in a wood a Piggy-wig stood
With a ring at the end of his nose,
His nose,
His nose,
With a ring at the end of his nose.

"Dear Pig, are you willing to sell for one shilling
Your ring?" Said the Piggy, "I will."

So they took it away, and were married next day
By the Turkey who lives on the hill.
They dined on mince, and slices of quince,
Which they ate with a runcible spoon;
And hand in hand, on the edge of the sand,
They danced by the light of the moon,
The moon,
The moon,
They danced by the light of the moon.

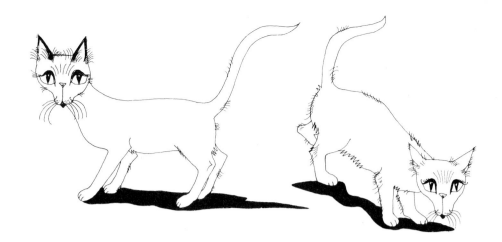

Cats no less liquid than their shadows

A. S. J. Tessimond

Cats, no less liquid than their shadows,
Offer no angles to the wind.
They slip, diminished, neat, through loopholes
Less than themselves; will not be pinned

To rules or routes for journeys; counter
Attack with non-resistance; twist
Enticing through the curving fingers

And leave an angered, empty fist.

They wait, obsequious as darkness
Quick to retire, quick to return;
Admit no aim or ethics; flatter
With reservations; will not learn

To answer to their names; are seldom
Truly owned till shot and skinned.
Cats, no less liquid than their shadows,
Offer no angles to the wind.

Six little mice

Six little mice sat down to spin;
Pussy passed by and she peeped in.
What are you doing, my little men?
Weaving coats for gentlemen.
Shall I come in and cut off your threads?
No, no, Mistress Pussy, you'd bite off our heads.
Oh, no, I'll not; I'll help you to spin.
That may be so, but you don't come in.

Cats!

Cats!
We're cats!
Lankies and skinnies and scruffies and fats;
Cats of all colours and cats of all sizes;
Nosers in dustbins and winners of prizes;
Stalkers on wallers and dozers up treesers;
Loungers on shelfers and scratchers of fleasers;
Long hairies, short hairies, chewed earers, proud tailers;
Mewers and purriers and spitters and wailers;
Burmese and Siamese, Persian and Manx cats, Marmalades,
Tabbies, Chinchillas and Van cats;
Strutters and sidlers and nuzzlers and liers;
Starers through windows and lazers near firers;
Chasers of mousies and catchers of rats;
We're cats!
Cats!

Cat purring

Keith Bosley

Cat purring
four furry paws
walking delicately between
flower stems
stalking butterflies

The robber kitten

R. M. Ballantyne

A kitten once to its mother said:
"I'll never more be good,
But I'll go and be a robber fierce,
And live in a dreary wood.
Wood, wood, wood,
And live in a dreary wood."

So off it went to the dreary wood,
And there it met a cock,
And blew its head, with a pistol, off,
Which gave it an awful shock.
Shock, shock, shock,
Which gave it an awful shock.

Soon after that it met a cat.
"Now, give to me your purse,
Or I'll shoot you through, and stab you too,
And kill you, which is worse.
Worse, worse, worse,
And kill you, which is worse."

22

It climbed a tree to rob a nest
Of young and tender owls;
But the branch broke off, and the kitten fell
With two tremendous howls.
Howls, howls, howls,
With two tremendous howls.

One day it met a Robber Dog,
And they sat down to drink;
The dog did joke, and laugh and sing,
Which made the kitten wink.
Wink, wink, wink,
Which made the kitten wink.

At last they quarrelled; then they fought,
Beneath the greenwood tree,
Till puss was felled with an awful club,
Most terrible to see.
See, see, see,
Most terrible to see.

When puss got up, its eye was shut,
And swelled, and black and blue;
Moreover, all its bones were sore,
So it began to mew.
Mew, mew, mew,
So it began to mew.

Then up it rose, and scratched its nose,
And went home very sad:
"Oh mother dear, behold me here;
I'll never more be bad.
Bad, bad, bad,
I'll never more be bad."

"Now, give to me your purse,
Or I'll shoot you through, and stab you too."

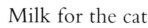

Milk for the cat

Harold Munro

When the tea is brought at five o'clock,
And all the neat curtains are drawn with care,
The little black cat with bright green eyes
Is suddenly purring there.

At first she pretends, having nothing to do,
She has come in merely to blink by the grate;
But, though tea may be late or the milk may be sour,
She is never late.

And presently her agate eyes
Take a soft large milky haze,
And her independent casual glance
Becomes a stiff hard gaze.

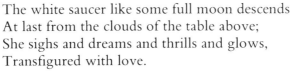

Then she stamps her claws or lifts her ears,
Or twists her tail and begins to stir,
Till suddenly all her lithe body becomes
One breathing trembling purr.

The children eat and wriggle and laugh;
The two old ladies stroke their silk:
But the cat is grown small and thin with desire,
Transformed to a creeping lust for milk.

The white saucer like some full moon descends
At last from the clouds of the table above;
She sighs and dreams and thrills and glows,
Transfigured with love.

She nestles over the shining rim,
Buries her chin in the creamy sea;
Her tail hangs loose; each drowsy paw
Is doubled under each bending knee.

A long dim ecstasy holds her life;
Her world is an infinite shapeless white,
Till her tongue has curled the last holy drop,
Then she sinks back into the night.

Draws and dips her body to heap
Her sleepy nerves in the great arm-chair,
Lies defeated and buried deep
Three or four hours unconscious there.

The Tyger

William Blake

Tyger! Tyger! burning bright
In the forests of the night,
What immortal hand or eye
Could frame thy fearful symmetry?

In what distant deeps or skies
Burnt the fire of thine eyes?
On what wings dare he aspire?
What the hand dare seize the fire?

And what shoulder, and what art,
Could twist the sinews of thy heart?
And when thy heart began to beat,
What dread hand? and what dread feet?

What the hammer? what the chain?
In what furnace was thy brain?
What the anvil? what dread grasp
Dare its deadly terrors clasp?

When the stars threw down their spears,
And watered Heaven with their tears,
Did he smile his work to see?
Did He who made the Lamb make thee?

Tyger! Tyger! burning bright
In the forests of the night,
What immortal hand or eye,
Dare frame thy fearful symmetry?

The lion

When man first went to look around
He saw a lion on the ground
The lion tried to give a smile
The man felt happy—for a while
Until he saw the lion's jaw
Full of teeth and looking for
Something good and fat to eat
So the man decided to retreat
The lion was only going to play
He'd already eaten once that day.

A kitten complains

Gobble, gobble, gobble, gobble
How those geese and ganders squabble!
Cluck, cluck, quack, quack, quack,
Ducks and chickens answer back.
Woof, woof, bark, bark, bark,
Puppies romp around and lark.
Moo go the cows, and the bull goes moo,
Oh what a hull-a-ba, hull-aba-loo.
The horse cries neigh and the sheep goes baa-a-a,
Squeak goes the trailer on the farmer's car.
The piglets are squealing, grunt, grunt goes the sow.
"Miaow," wails black pussy,
Miaow, what a row,
There's such a commotion, how can a cat sleep?
With the noise of the dogs and the cows and the sheep
And the hens and the ducks
And the ganders and geese.

And the squeak of the trailer that's needing some grease,
With the moo of the bull and the neigh of the horse
And the shrieking of piglets to make matters worse.
But—it's no use complaining, for nobody hears
So I'll hide in the loft and stuff hay in my ears.
Up there, warm and cosy in my coat of fur,
I'll practise *my* solo, "miaow, purr, purr, purr."

This is the Cat

This is the Cat
That killed the Cock,
For waking her
At five o'clock.

When the cat

When the cat winketh
Little wots the mouse
What the cat thinketh.

Alice and the Cheshire Cat

Lewis Carroll

Alice was just beginning to think to herself, 'Now, what am I to do with this creature when I get it home?' when it grunted again, so violently, that she looked down into its face in some alarm. This time there could be *no* mistake about it: it was neither more nor less than a pig, and she felt that it would be quite absurd for her to carry it any further.

So she set the little creature down, and felt quite relieved to see it trot quietly away into the wood. 'If it had grown up,' she said to herself, 'it would have made a dreadfully ugly child: but it makes rather a handsome pig, I think.' And she began thinking over other children she knew, who might do very well as pigs, and was just saying to herself, 'if one only knew the right way to change them—' when she was a little startled by seeing the Cheshire Cat sitting on a bough of a tree a few yards off.

The Cat only grinned when it saw Alice. It looked good-natured, she thought: still it had *very* long claws and a great many teeth, so she felt that it ought to be treated with respect.

'Cheshire Puss,' she began, rather timidly, as she did not at all know whether it would like the name: however, it only grinned a little wider. 'Come, it's pleased so far,' thought Alice, and she went on. 'Would you tell me please, which way I ought to go from here?'

'That depends a good deal on where you want to get to,' said the Cat.

'I don't much care where—' said Alice.

'Then it doesn't matter which way you go,' said the Cat.

'—so long as I get *somewhere*,' Alice added as an explanation.

'Oh, you're sure to do that,' said the Cat, 'if you only walk long enough.'

Alice felt that this could not be denied, so she tried another question. 'What sort of people live about here?'

'In *that* direction,' the Cat said, waving its right paw round, 'lives a Hatter: and in *that* direction,' waving the other paw, 'lives a March Hare. Visit either you like: they're both mad.'

'But I don't want to go among mad people,' Alice remarked.

'Oh, you can't help that,' said the Cat: 'we're all mad here. I'm mad. You're mad.'

'How do you know I'm mad?' said Alice.

'You must be,' said the Cat, 'or you wouldn't have come here.'

Alice didn't think that proved it at all; however, she went on. 'And how do you know that you're mad?'

'To begin with,' said the Cat, 'a dog's not mad. You grant that?'

'I suppose so,' said Alice.

'Well, then,' the Cat went on, 'you see a dog growls when it's angry, and wags its tail when it's pleased. Now *I* growl when I'm pleased, and wag my tail when I'm angry. Therefore I'm mad.'

'*I* call it purring, not growling,' said Alice.

'Call it what you like,' said the Cat. 'Do you play croquet with the Queen today?'

'I should like it very much,' said Alice, 'but I haven't been invited yet.'

'You'll see me there,' said the Cat and vanished.

Alice was not much surprised at this, she was getting so used to queer things happening. While she was looking at the place where it had been, it suddenly appeared again.

'By-the-bye, what became of the baby?' said the Cat. 'I'd nearly forgotten to ask.'

'It turned into a pig,' Alice quietly said, just as if it had come back in a natural way.

"I thought it would,' said the Cat, and vanished again.

Alice waited a little, half expecting to see it again, but it did not appear, and after a minute or two she walked on in the direction in which the March Hare was said to live. 'I've seen hatters before,' she said to herself; 'the March Hare will be much the most interesting, and perhaps as this is May, it won't be raving mad—at least not so mad as it was in March.' As she said this, she looked up, and there was the Cat again, sitting on the branch of a tree.

'Did you say pig, or fig?' said the Cat.

'I said pig,' replied Alice; 'and I wish you wouldn't keep appearing and vanishing so suddenly: you make one quite giddy.'

'All right,' said the Cat; and this time it vanished quite slowly, beginning with the end of the tail, and ending with the grin, which remained some time after the rest of it had gone.

'Well! I've often seen a cat without a grin,' thought Alice; 'but a grin without a cat! It's the most curious thing I ever saw in all my life.'

She had not gone much farther before she came in sight of the house of the March Hare: she thought it must be the right house, because the chimneys were shaped like ears and the roof was thatched with fur. It was so large a house, that she did not like to go nearer till she had nibbled some more of the left-hand bit of mushroom, and raised herself, to about two feet high: even then she walked up towards it rather timidly, saying to herself, 'Suppose it should be raving mad after all! I almost wish I'd gone to see the Hatter instead!'

From *Alice's Adventures in Wonderland*

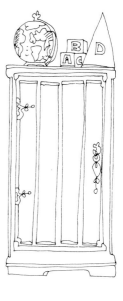

A, B, C, tumble down dee

A, B, C, tumble down dee,
The cat's in the cupboard,
And can't see me.

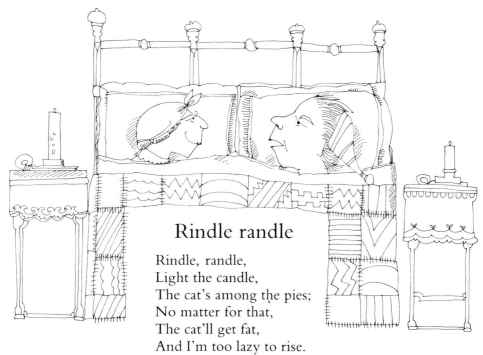

Rindle randle

Rindle, randle,
Light the candle,
The cat's among the pies;
No matter for that,
The cat'll get fat,
And I'm too lazy to rise.

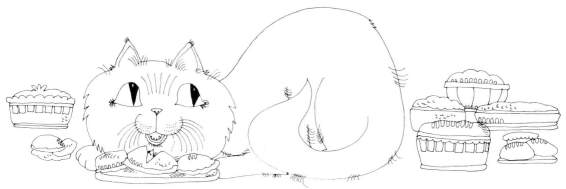

Under-the-table manners

It's very hard to be polite
If you're a cat.
When other folks are up at table
Eating all that they are able,
You are down upon the mat
If you're a cat.

You're expected just to sit
If you're a cat.
Not to let them know you're there
By scratching at the chair,
Or a light, respected pat
If you're a cat.

You are not to make a fuss
If you're a cat.
Tho' there's fish upon the plate
You're expected just to wait,
Wait politely on the mat
If you're a cat.

Kit's cradle

Juliana Horatia Ewing

They've taken the cosy bed away
That I made myself with the Shetland shawl,
And set me a hamper of scratchy hay,
By that great black stove in the entrance hall.

I won't sleep there; I'm resolved on that!
They may think I will, but they little know
There's a soft persistence about a cat
That even a little kitten can show.

I wish I knew what to do but pout,
And spit at the dogs and refuse my tea;
My fur's feeling rough, and I rather doubt
Whether stolen sausage agrees with me.

On the drawing-room soft they've closed the door,
They've turned me out of the easy-chairs;
I wonder it never struck me before
That they make their beds for themselves upstairs.

I've found a crib where they won't find me,
Though they're crying "Kitty!" all over the house.
Hunt for the Slipper! and riddle-my-ree!
A cat can keep as still as a mouse.

It's rather unwise perhaps to purr,
But they'll never think of the wardrobe-shelves.
I'm happy in every hair of my fur;
They may keep the hamper and hay themselves.

Breakfast and puss

Jane and Ann Taylor

Here's my baby's bread and milk,
For her lip as soft as silk;
Here's the basin clean and neat,
Here's the spoon of silver sweet,
Here's the stool, and here's the chair,
For my little lady fair.

No, you must not spill it out,
And drop the bread and milk about;
But let it stand before you flat,
And pray remember pussy-cat;
Poor old pussy-cat, that purrs
All so patiently for hers.

True, she runs about the house,
Catching now and then a mouse;
But, though she thinks it very nice,
That only makes a tiny slice:
So don't forget that you should stop,
And leave poor puss a little drop.

Miss Jane

Miss Jane had a bag,
And a mouse was in it,
She opened the bag,
He was out in a minute;
The Cat saw him jump,
And run under the table,
And the dog said, catch him, puss,
Soon as you're able.

Good morning, cat

Myra Cohn Livingston

Good morning, cat,
you're in my yard
and sniffing for a mouse;
you might as well give up—because
he's hiding in the house.

The cat and the moon

W. B. Yeats

The cat went here and there
And the moon spun round like a top,
And the nearest kin of the moon,
The creeping cat, looked up.
Black Minnaloushe stared at the moon,
For, wander and wail as he would,
The pure cold light in the sky
Troubled his animal blood.
Minnaloushe runs in the grass
Lifting his delicate feet.
Do you dance, Minnaloushe, do you dance?
When two close kindred meet,
What better than call a dance?
Maybe the moon may learn,
Tired of that courtly fashion,
A new dance turn.
Minnaloushe creeps through the grass
From moonlit place to place,
The sacred moon overhead
Has taken a new phase.
Does Minnaloushe know that his pupils
Will pass from change to change,
And that from round to crescent,
From crescent to round they range?
Minnaloushe creeps through the grass
Alone, important and wise,
And lifts to the changing moon
His changing eyes.

A Cat

Edward Thomas

She had a name among the children;
But no one loved though someone owned
Her, locked her out of doors at bedtime
And had her kittens duly drowned.

In Spring, nevertheless, this cat
Ate blackbirds, thrushes, nightingales,
And birds of bright voice and plume and flight,
As well as scraps from neighbours' pails.

I loathed and hated her for this;
One speckle on a thrush's breast
Was worth a million such; and yet
She lived long, till God gave her rest.

Cat

Mary Britton Miller

The black cat yawns,
Opens her jaws,
Stretches her legs,
And shows her claws.

Then she gets up
And stands on four
Long stiff legs
And yawns some more.

She shows her sharp teeth,
She stretches her lip,
Her slice of a tongue
Turns at the tip.

Lifting herself
On her delicate toes,
She arches her back
As high as it goes.

She lets herself down
With particular care,
And pads away
With her tail in the air.

44

Rat a tat tat

Rat a tat tat, who is that?
Only grandma's pussy cat.
What do you want?
A pint of milk.
Where's your money?
In my pocket.
Where's your pocket?
I forgot it.
O you silly pussy cat!

Pussy cat, pussy cat

Pussy cat, pussy cat, where have you been?
I've been to London to look at the queen.
Pussy cat, pussy cat, what did you there?
I frightened a little mouse under her chair.

Sing, sing, what shall I sing

Sing, sing, what shall I sing?
The cat's run away with the pudding-bag string.
Do, do, what shall I do?
The dog has bitten it right in two!

There was a crooked man

There was a crooked man, and he went a crooked mile
He found a crooked sixpence against a crooked stile
He bought a crooked cat, which caught a crooked mouse
And they all lived together in a little crooked house.

Lickety, splickety, and the old Tom Cat

Lickety, splickety, very pernickety
Mrs O'Connolly hustles along on her
Rickety bicycle, cold as an icicle,
Treadalling pedalling meddling on!

and the old
tom cat
stretches slowly
by the fire.

What can the matter be, Mrs O'Rafferty
Falling all over herself in her worry to
Get to the baker and pick out a cake for a
Jolly-good-gobble-it-down-in-a-hurry!

and the old
tom cat
pads slowly
up the stairs.

Oh what a calamity, Mrs O'Flamity
Falls out the window on top of a barrow—
it tumbles and jumbles up Mrs O'Connolly—
Mrs O'Rafferty slips down a narrow
Gap down by the gutter and falls in a pothole.
Oh mercy! The poor silly thing is in agony!
Mrs O'Connolly's under a Jag! Any
witnesses please to this dreadful calamity
Come to the Polis and please bring a bottle!

And the old
tom cat
rolls over, smiles, and sleeps.

The cat sat asleep

The cat sat asleep by the side of the fire,
The mistress snored loud as a pig;
Jack took up his fiddle by Jenny's desire,
And struck up a bit of a jig.

I doot, I doot

I doot, I doot, my fire's out,
And my little dog's not at home;
I'll saddle my cat, I'll bridle my cat,
And bring my little dog home;
A hapenny pudding, a hapenny pie,
Stand ye there out by.

Two cats

Samuel Marshak

Two cats?—
Why! that's
Eight paws,
Two tails and
Forty claws.

Chitterabob

There was a man, and his name was Dob,
And he had a wife, and her name was Mob,
And he had a dog, and he called it Cob,
And she had a cat, called Chitterabob.
Cob, says Dob,
Chitterabob, says Mob.
Cob was Dob's dog,
Chitterabob Mob's cat.

A cat came dancing

A cat came dancing out of a barn
With a pair of bag-pipes under her arm;
She could sing nothing but, Fiddle cum fee,
The mouse has married the bumble-bee.
Pipe, cat; dance, mouse;
We'll have a wedding at our good house.

Hey diddle diddle

Hey diddle diddle,
The cat and fiddle,
The cow jumped over the moon,
The little dog laughed
To see such sport,
And the dish ran away with the spoon.

Lingle, lingle

Lingle, lingle, lang tang,
Our cat's dead!
What did she die with?
With a sore head!
All you that kent her,
When she was alive,
Come to her burial.

Marigold

Richard Garnett

She moved through the garden in glory, because
She had very long claws at the end of her paws.
Her back was arched, her tail was high,
A green fire glared in her vivid eye;
And all the Toms, though never so bold,
Quailed at the martial Marigold.

The cat of cats

William Brighty Rands

I am the cat of cats. I am
The everlasting cat!
Cunning, and old, and sleek as jam,
The everlasting cat!
I hunt the vermin in the night—
The everlasting cat!
For I see best without the light—
The everlasting cat!

Pussy at the fireside

Pussy at the fireside suppin' up brose,
Down came a cinder and burned pussy's nose.
Oh, said pussy, that's not fair.
Well, said the cinder, you shouldn't be there.

Pussy cat mew

Pussy cat mew jumped over a coal,
And in her best petticoat burnt a great hole;
Pussy cat mew shall have no more milk,
Till her best petticoat's mended with silk.

The mysterious cat

Vachel Lindsay

I saw a proud, mysterious cat
I saw a proud, mysterious cat,
Too proud to catch a mouse or rat—

Mew, mew, mew.

But catnip she would eat, and purr,
But catnip she would eat, and purr.
And goldfish she did much prefer—
Mew, mew, mew.

I saw a cat—'twas but a dream,
I saw a cat—'twas but a dream
Who scorned the slave that brought her cream—
Mew, mew, mew.

Unless the slave were dressed in style,
Unless the slave were dressed in style
And knelt before her all the while—
Mew, mew, mew.

Did you ever hear of a thing like that?
Did you ever hear of a thing like that?
Did you ever hear of a thing like that?
Oh, what a proud mysterious cat.
Oh, what a proud mysterious cat.
Oh, what a proud mysterious cat.
Mew . . . Mew . . . Mew.

If the little mice peep,
They'll think I'm asleep.''

Pussy-Cat

Mrs Hawkshaw

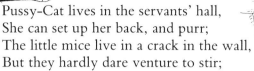

Pussy-Cat lives in the servants' hall,
She can set up her back, and purr;
The little mice live in a crack in the wall,
But they hardly dare venture to stir;

For whenever they think of taking the air,
Or filling their little maws,
The Pussy-Cat says: "Come out, if you dare;
I will catch you all with my claws."

Scrabble, scrabble, scrabble, went all the little mice
For they smelt the Cheshire cheese;
The Pussy-Cat said: "It smells very nice,
Now do come out, if you please."

"Squeak," said the little Mouse; "Squeak, squeak,"
Said all the young ones too;
"We never creep out when cats are about,
Because we're afraid of you."

So the cunning old Cat lay down on a mat
By the fire in the servants' hall;
"If the little Mice peep, they'll think I'm asleep"
So she rolled herself up like a ball.

"Squeak," said the little Mouse, "we'll creep out
And eat some Cheshire cheese,
That silly old cat is asleep on the mat,
And we may sup at our ease."

Nibble, nibble, nibble, went all the little mice,
And they licked their little paws;
Then the cunning old cat sprang up from the mat
And caught them all with her claws.

Three little kittens

Three little kittens
They lost their mittens
And they began to cry,
Oh, mother dear, we sadly fear
Our mittens we have lost.
What! Lost your mittens,
You naughty kittens!
Then you shall have no pie.
Mee-ow, mee-ow, mee-ow.
No, you shall have no pie.

The three little kittens,
They found their mittens,
And they began to cry,
Oh, mother dear, see here, see here,
Our mittens we have found.
Put on your mittens,
You silly kittens,
And you shall have some pie.
Purr-r, purr-r, purr-r,
Oh, let us have some pie.

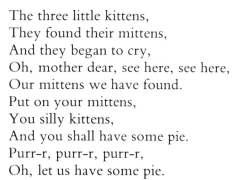

Two little kittens, one stormy night,
Began to quarrel and then to fight.

Two little kittens

Two little kittens, one stormy night,
Began to quarrel, and then to fight;
One had a mouse, the other had none,
And that's the way the quarrel begun.

"I'll have that mouse," said the biggest cat;
"You'll have that mouse? We'll see about that!"
"I *will* have that mouse," said the eldest son;
"You *shan't* have the mouse," said the little one.

I told you before 'twas a stormy night;
When these two little kittens began to fight;
The old woman seized her sweeping broom,
And swept the two kittens right out of the room.

The ground was covered with frost and snow,
And the two little kittens had nowhere to go;
So they laid them down on the mat at the door,
While the old woman finished sweeping the floor.

Then they crept in, as quiet as mice,
All wet with the snow, and as cold as ice,
For they found it was better, that stormy night,
To lie down and sleep than to quarrel and fight.

A dog and a cat

A dog and a cat went out together
To see some friends just out of town,
Said the cat to the dog,
"What d'ye think of the weather?"
"I think, ma'am, the rain will come down;
But don't be alarmed, for I've an umbrella
That will shelter us both,"
Said this amiable fellow.

We are all in the dumps

We are all in the dumps,
For diamonds are trumps;
The kittens are gone to St Paul's.
The babies are bit,
The Moon's in a fit,
And the houses are built without walls.

Puss in Boots

Charles Perrault

A Miller, dying, divided all his property among his three sons. This was a very simple matter as he had nothing much to leave them: to his eldest son went his mill, to the second his ass, while the third was obliged to be content with his cat, at which he grumbled, 'There is nothing left for me but to kill the cat, eat him and make a coat out of his skin.'

The cat sat up on his four paws and gravely said, 'Master, you have but to give me a sack and a pair of boots and you will find me much more useful to you alive.'

The young man was so surprised that he trusted the cat. So Puss got his boots and, with his sack over his shoulder, he made for a nearby rabbit warren. There, he put down the sack, with some bran and lettuce inside, and waited for some fine fat unsuspecting rabbit to be lured into it. This happened very shortly, and when one put his head into the sack Master Puss drew tight the cords and trapped it. Then he marched directly to the Palace and demanded to see the King.

'Sire,' he said to his Majesty, 'here is a magnificent rabbit offered humbly to you by my master, the Marquis of Carabas.' And the King, being partial to rabbit pie, graciously accepted.

The next day Puss caught two splendid fat partridges, which he offered to the King with the same message. His Majesty, being equally fond of partridge, ordered that the cat be made welcome in the Royal Kitchens where, between mouthfuls, Puss cunningly talked of his master and his fine lands.

Hearing that the King and his beautiful daughter were to take a drive past the river, Puss went back to his master and said, 'Your fortune is made! Go and bathe in the river and leave the rest to me. Only remember, you are the Marquis of Carabas!'

'It's all the same to me,' said the Miller. While he was bathing, the King and his court drove by and heard loud cries of 'Help! My lord the Marquis of Carabas is drowning!'

Recognizing the cat, the King ordered his guards to rescue the Marquis and while they did so Puss told the King a pitiful story of how thieves had stolen his master's clothing while he was bathing. Upon this, the King sent back to the Palace for an elegant supply of clothes.

Once dressed and looking as a young and handsome Marquis should, the Miller presented himself to the King, who received him courteously, and to the Princess, who admired him very much. Indeed, so much that she insisted the young man rode with them in the Royal Carriage.

The cat, delighted with his scheme, ran on until he met some reapers. 'If you do not say all these lands belong to my lord the Marquis of Carabas, you shall be chopped as small as mince meat.' He said it with such force that when the King drove past and asked to whom belonged such a fine crop of hay, the trembling reapers answered 'The Marquis of Carabas!'

On the cat ran until he arrived at a great castle where dwelt a tyrannical Ogre. Puss marched through the gates and demanded to see him. 'I have heard it told,' he said boldly to the Ogre, 'that you can change yourself into any beast you choose—even a lion!'

'That is true,' boasted the Ogre, 'and lest you doubt it . . .' The cat was so frightened by the lion he saw before him that he jumped onto the castle roof—most inconvenient on account of his boots—until the Ogre returned to his original form.

'But sir,' Puss ventured to say, 'I do not suppose it can be so easy to become as small as a mouse?'

'Easy!' boasted the Ogre. Immediately the cat saw the little mouse on the floor, he did the very best a cat could do and sprang upon it and gobbled it up. And there was the end of the Ogre.

By the time the King arrived, the cat was standing at the gates to welcome him to the castle of the Marquis of Carabas.

'What!' cried his Majesty, much surprised. 'Truly, Marquis, does this too belong to you?'

The Marquis, smiling, offered the King and the Princess his humble hospitality, for he had already achieved the manner of court, and Puss led them to a magnificent banquet.

Before the banquet was over, the King, charmed with the good qualities of the Marquis, and likewise of the wine, said, 'It rests with you, Marquis, whether you will not become my son-in-law.'

The Marquis, of course, was pleased to agree, and the Princess was equally pleased that he did so. And the cat had nevermore need to chase mice, *except for his own diversion.*

The ratcatcher and cats

John Gay

The rats by night such mischief did,
Betty was ev'ry morning chid:
They undermin'd whole sides of bacon,
Her cheese was sapp'd, her tarts were taken,
Her pasties, fenc'd with thickest paste,
Were all demolish'd and laid waste.
She curst the cat for want of duty,
Who left her foes a constant booty.
An Engineer, of noted skill,
Engag'd to stop the growing ill.
From room to room he now surveys
Their haunts, their works, their secret ways.
Finds where they 'scape an ambuscade,
And whence the nightly sally's made.
An envious Cat, from place to place,
Unseen, attends his silent pace,
She saw that if his trade went on,
The purring race must be undone,
So, secretly removes his baits,
And ev'ry stratagem defeats.
Again he sets the poison'd toils,
And puss again the labour foils.
What foe (to frustrate my designs)
My schemes thus nightly undermines?
Incens'd, he cries: this very hour
The wretch shall bleed beneath my power.
So said. A pond'rous trap he brought,
And in the fact poor puss was caught.
Smuggler, says he, thou shalt be made

A victim to our loss of trade.
The captive Cat with piteous mews
For pardon, life and freedom sues.
A sister of the science spare,
One int'rest is our common care.
What insolence! the man reply'd,
Shall cats with us the game divide?
Were all your interloping band
Extinguish'd, or expell'd the land,
We Rat-catchers might raise our fees,
Sole guardians of a nation's cheese!
A Cat, who saw the lifted knife,
Thus spoke, and sav'd her sister's life.
In ev'ry age and clime we see,
Two of a trade can ne'er agree,
Each hates his neighbour for encroaching;
Squire stigmatizes squire for poaching;
Beauties with beauties are in arms,
And scandal pelts each other's charms;
Kings too their neighbour kings dethrone,
In hope to make the world their own.
But let us limit our desires,
Not war like beauties, kings and squires,
For though we both one prey pursue,
There's game enough for us and you.

From *Fables*

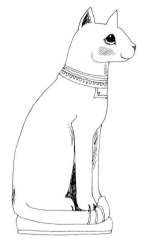

Suttee of the cats

George Rawlinson

The number of domestic animals in Egypt is very great, and would be still greater were it not for what befalls the cats. As the females, when they have kittened, no longer seek the company of the males, these last, to obtain once more their companionship, practise a curious artifice. They seize the kittens, carry them off, and kill them, but do not eat them afterwards. Upon this the females, being deprived of their young, and longing to supply their place, seek the males once more, since they are particularly fond of their offspring. On every occasion of a fire in Egypt the strangest prodigy occurs with the cats. The inhabitants allow the fire to rage as it pleases, while they stand about at intervals and watch these animals which, slipping by the men or else leaping over them, rush headlong into the flames. When this happens, the Egyptians are in deep affliction. If a cat dies in a private house by a natural death, all the inmates of the house shave their eyebrows. . . . The cats on their decease are taken to the city of Bubastis, where they are embalmed, after which they are buried in certain sacred repositories.

From the translation of Second Book of the History of Herodotus, entitled *Euterpe*

Sir Roger de Coverley and Moll White

Joseph Addison

This account raised my curiosity so far that I begged my friend Sir
Roger to go with me into her hovel, which stood in a solitary corner
under the side of the wood. Upon our first entering Sir Roger winked
to me and pointed at something that stood behind the door, which,
upon looking that way I discovered to be an old broomstaff. At the
same time he whispered me in the ear, to take notice of a tabby cat that
sat in the chimney-corner, which, as the old knight told me, lay under
as bad a report as Moll White herself, for besides that Moll was said
often to accompany her in the same shape, the cat is reported to have
spoken twice or thrice in her life and to have played several pranks
above the capacity of an ordinary cat.

Extract from paper No. 117 contributed to *The Spectator*

The master's cat

Mary Dickens

One evening we were all, except father, going to a ball, and when we started, we left 'the master' and his cat in the drawing-room together. 'The Master' was reading at a small table; suddenly the candle went out. My father, who was much interested in his book, relighted the candle, stroked the cat, who was looking at him pathetically he noticed, and continued his reading. A few minutes later, as the light became dim, he looked up just in time to see puss deliberately put out the candle with his paw, and then look appealingly at him. This second and unmistakable hint was not disregarded and puss was given the petting he craved.

From *My Father as I Recall Him*
(by Mary, daughter of Charles Dickens)

The cat

W. H. Davies

Within that porch across the way,
I see two naked eyes this night;
Two eyes that neither shut nor blink,
Searching my face with a green light.

But cats to me are strange so strange—
I cannot sleep if one is near,
And though I'm sure I see those eyes,
I'm not so sure a body's there!

Sam Weller and Mr Brooks's cats

Charles Dickens

'I lodged in the same house vith a pieman once, sir, and a wery nice man he was—reg'lar clever chap, too—make pies out o' anything, he could. "What a number o' cats you keep, Mr Brooks," says I, when I'd got intimate with him. "Ah," says he, "I do—a good many," says he. "You must be wery fond o' cats," says I. "Other people is," says he, a-winkin' at me; "they ain't in season till the winter though," says he. "Not in season!" says I. "No," says he, "fruits is in, cats is out." "Why, what do you mean?" says I. "Mean?" says he. "That I'll never be a party to the combination o' the butchers, to keep up the price o' meat," says he. "Mr Weller," says he, a-squeezing my hand wery hard, and vispering in my ear—"don't mention this here agin —but it's the seasonin' as does it. They're all made o' them noble animals," says he, a-pointin' to a wery nice little tabby kitten, "and I seasons 'em for beefsteak, weal, or kidney, 'cording to the demand. And more than that," says he, "I can make a weal a beef-steak, or a beef-steak a kidney, or any one on 'em a mutton, at a minute's notice, just as the market changes, and appetites wary!"'

'He must have been a very ingenious young man, that, Sam,' said Mr Pickwick, with a slight shudder.

From *The Pickwick Papers*

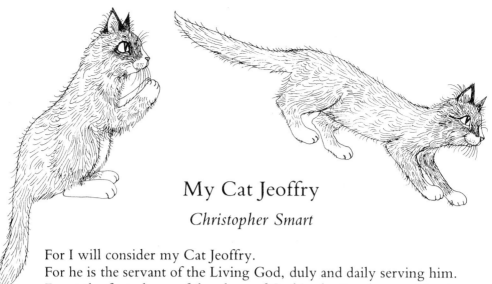

My Cat Jeoffry

Christopher Smart

For I will consider my Cat Jeoffry.
For he is the servant of the Living God, duly and daily serving him.
For at the first glance of the glory of God in the East he worships in his way.
For is this done by wreathing his body seven times round with elegant quickness.
For then he leaps up to catch the musk, which is the blessing of God upon his prayer.
For he rolls upon prank to work it in.
For having done duty and received blessing he begins to consider himself.
For this he performs in ten degrees.
For first he looks upon his fore-paws to see if they are clean.
For secondly he kicks up behind to clear away there.
For thirdly he works it upon stretch with the fore-paws extended.
For fourthly he sharpens his paws by wood.
For fifthly he washes himself.
For sixthly he rolls upon wash.
For seventhly he fleas himself, that he may not be interrupted upon the beat.
For eighthly he rubs himself against a post.
For ninthly he looks up for his instructions.
For tenthly he goes in quest of food.

For having consider'd God and himself he will consider his
neighbour.
For if he meets another cat he will kiss her in kindness.
For when he takes his prey he plays with it to give it [a] chance.
For one mouse in seven escapes by his dallying.
For when his day's work is done his business more properly begins.
For he keeps the Lord's watch in the night against the adversary.
For he counteracts the powers of darkness by his electrical skin &
glaring eyes.
For he counteracts the Devil, who is death, by brisking about the
life.
For in his morning orisons he loves the sun and the sun loves him.
For he is of the tribe of Tiger.
For the Cherub Cat is a term of the Angel Tiger.
For he has the subtlety and hissing of a serpent, which in goodness
he suppresses.
For he will not do destruction, if he is well-fed, neither will he spit
without provocation.
For he purrs in thankfulness, when God tells him he's a good Cat.
For he is an instrument for the children to learn benevolence upon.
For every house is incompleat without him & a blessing is lacking
in the spirit.

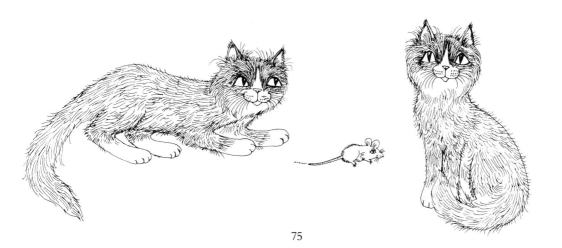

Mrs Forrester's lace

Mrs Gaskell

. . . I treasure up my lace very much. . . . I always wash it myself. And once it had a narrow escape. Of course, your ladyship knows that such lace must never be starched or ironed. Some people wash it in sugar and water, and some in coffee, to make it the right yellow colour; but I myself have a very good receipt for washing it in milk, which stiffens it enough and gives it a very good creamy colour. Well, ma'am, I had tacked it together (and the beauty of this fine lace is that, when it is wet, it goes into a very little space), and put it to soak in milk, when, unfortunately, I left the room; on my return I found pussy on the table, looking very like a thief, but gulping very uncomfortably, as if she was half-choked with something she wanted to swallow and could not. And would you believe it? At first I pitied her, and said 'Poor pussy! Poor pussy!' till, all at once, I looked and saw the cup of milk empty—cleaned out! 'You naughty cat!' said I; and I believe I was provoked enough to give her a slap, which did no good, but only helped the lace down—just as one slaps a choking child on the back. I could have cried, I was so vexed; but I determined I would not give the lace up without a struggle for it. I hoped the lace might disagree with her, at any rate; but it would have been too much for Job, if he had seen, as I did, that cat come in, quite placid and purring, not a quarter of an hour after, and almost expecting to be stroked. 'No, pussy!' said I, 'if you have any conscience you ought not to expect that!' And then a thought struck me; and I rang the bell for my maid,

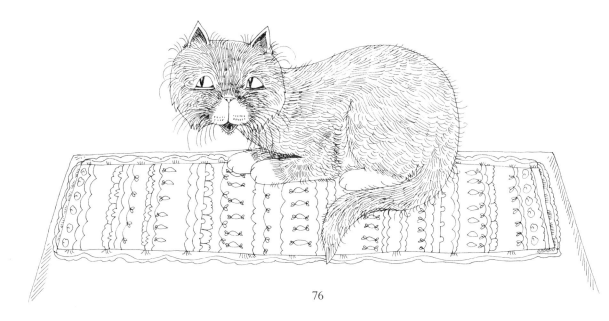

and sent her to Mr Hoggins, with my compliments, and would he be kind enough to lend me one of his top-boots for an hour? I did not think there was anything odd in the message; but Jenny said the young men in the surgery laughed as if they would be ill at my wanting a top-boot. When it came, Jenny and I put pussy in, with her fore-feet straight down, so that they were fastened, and could not scratch, and we gave her a teaspoonful of currant-jelly in which (your ladyship must excuse me) I had mixed some tartar emetic. I shall never forget how anxious I was for the next half-hour. I took pussy to my own room, and spread a clean towel on the floor. I could have kissed her when she returned the lace to sight, very much as it had gone down. Jenny had boiling water ready, and we soaked it and soaked it, and spread it on a lavender-bush in the sun before I could touch it again, even to put it in milk. But now your ladyship would never guess that it had been in pussy's inside.

From *Cranford*

The cats and the viper

William Cowper

Passing from the green-house into the barn I saw three kittens (we have so many in our retinue) looking with fixed attention at something which lay on the threshold of a door curled up. I took but little notice of them at first but a loud hiss engaged me to attend more closely, when behold, a viper! The largest I remember to have seen, rearing itself, darting its forked tongue and ejaculating the aforementioned hiss at the nose of a kitten almost in contact with his lips. I ran into the hall for a hoe with a long handle, with which I intended to assail him, and returning in a few seconds missed him: he was gone and I feared had escaped me. Still however the kitten sat watching immovably in the same spot. I concluded therefore that, sliding between the door and the threshold, he had found his way out of the garden into the yard. I went round immediately and there found him in close conversation with the old cat, whose curiosity being excited by so novel an experience, inclined her to pat his head repeatedly with her fore-foot; with her claws, however, sheathed, and not in anger, but in the way of philosophical enquiry and examination.

To prevent her falling a victim to so laudable an exercise of her talents, I interposed in a moment with the hoe and performed upon him an act of decapitation which, though not immediately mortal, proved so in the end. Had he slid into the passages, where it is dark, or had he, when in the yard, met no interruption from the cat and secreted himself in one of the outhouses, it is hardly possible but that some of the family must have been bitten.

letter to the Rev. William Unwin, 3 August 1782

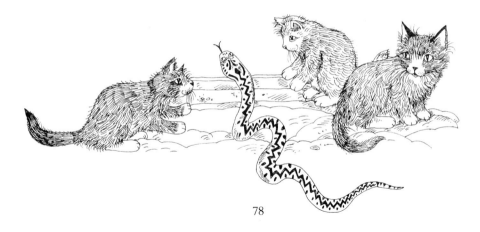

The old woman and her cats

John Gay

Who friendship with a knave hath made
Is judg'd a partner in the trade.
The matron, who conducts abroad
A willing nymph, is thought a bawd;
And if a modest girl is seen
With one who cures a lover's spleen,
We guess her, not extremely nice,
And only wish to know her price.
'Tis thus, that on the choice of friends
Our good or evil name depends.

A wrinkled hag, of wicked fame,
Beside a little smoky flame
Sat hov'ring, pinch'd with age and frost;
Her shrivell'd hands, with veins embost,
Upon her knees her weight sustains,
While palsy shook her crazy brains;
She mumbles forth her backward prayers,
An untam'd scold of fourscore years.
About her swarm'd a num'rous brood
Of Cats, who lank with hunger mew'd.

Teaz'd with their cries her choler grew,
And thus she sputter'd. Hence, ye crew.
Fool that I was, to entertain
Such imps, such fiends, a hellish train!
Had ye been never hous'd and nurs't
I, for a witch, had ne'er been curst.
To you I owe, that crouds of boys
Worry me with eternal noise;
Straws laid across my pace retard,
The horse-shoe's nail'd (each threshold's guard)
The stunted broom the wenches hide,
For fear that I should up and ride;
They stick with pins my bleeding seat,
And bid me shew my secret teat.

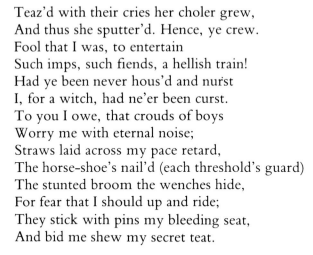

To hear you prate would vex a saint,
Who hath most reason of complaint?
Replies a Cat. Let's come to proof.
Had we ne'er starved beneath your roof.
We had, like others of our race,
In credit liv'd, as beasts of chace.
'Tis infamy to serve a hag;
Cats are thought imps, her broom a nag;
And boys against our lives combine,
Because, 'tis said, your cats have nine.

From *Fables*

Tragedy at sea

Henry Fielding

Thursday, July 11th, 1754. A most tragical incident fell out this day at sea. While the ship was under sail, but making as will appear no great way, a kitten, one of four of the feline inhabitants of the cabin, fell from the window into the water: an alarm was immediately given to the captain, who was then upon deck, and received it with the utmost concern and many bitter oaths. He immediately gave orders to the steersman in favour of the poor thing, as he called it; the sails were instantly slackened, and all hands, as the phrase is, employed to recover the poor animal. I was, I own, extremely surprised at all this; less indeed at the captain's extreme tenderness than at his conceiving any possibility of success; for if puss had had nine thousand instead of nine lives, I concluded they had been all lost. The boatswain, however, had more sanguine hopes, for having stripped himself of his jacket, breeches and shirt, he leaped boldly into the water, and to my great astonishment, in a few minutes returned to the ship, bearing the motionless animal in his mouth. Nor was this, I observed, a matter of such great difficulty as it appeared to my ignorance, and possibly may seem to that of my fresh-water reader. The kitten was now exposed to air and sun on the deck, where its life, of which it retained no symptoms, was despaired of by all.

But as I have, perhaps, a little too wantonly endeavoured to raise the tender passions of my readers in this narrative, I should think myself unpardonable if I concluded it without giving them the satisfaction of hearing that the kitten at last recovered, to the great joy of the good captain, but to the great disappointment of some of the sailors, who asserted that the drowning cat was the very surest way of raising a favourable wind; a supposition of which, though we have heard several plausible accounts, we will not presume to assign the true original reason. From *A Voyage to Lisbon*

The lover whose Mistresse feared a mouse

George Turberville

If I might alter kind,
What, think you, I would bee?
Nor Fish, nor Foule, nor Fle, nor Frog,
Nor Squirril on the Tree;
The Fish the Hooke, the Foule
The lymed Twig doth catch,
The Fle the Finger, and the Frog
The Bustard doth dispatch.

The Squirril thinking nought,
That feately cracks the Nut,
The greedie Goshawke wanting pray
In dread of Death doth put;
But scorning all these kindes,
I would become a Cat,
To combat with the creeping Mouse,
And scratch the screeking Rat.

I would be present, aye,
And at my Ladie's call;
To gard her from the fearfull Mouse,
In Parlour and in Hall;
In Kitchen, for his Lyfe,
He should not shew his head;
The Peare in Poke should lie untoucht
When shee were gone to Bed.
The Mouse should stand in Feare,
So should the squeaking Rat;
And this would I do if I were
Converted to a Cat.

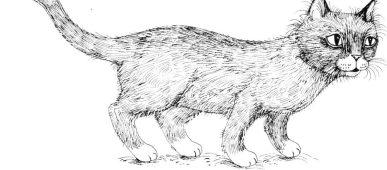

To A Cat
A. C. Swinburne

To a cat

A. C. Swinburne

Stately, kindly, lordly friend,
Condescend

Here to sit by me, and turn
Glorious eyes that smile and burn,
Golden eyes, love's lustrous meed,
On the golden page I read.

All your wondrous wealth of hair,
Dark and fair,
Silken-shaggy, soft and bright
As the clouds and beams of night,
Pays my reverent hand's caress
Back with friendlier gentleness.

Dogs may fawn on all and some
As they come;
You, a friend of loftier mind,
Answer friends alone in kind.
Just your foot upon my hand
Softly bids it understand.

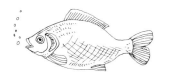
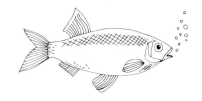

A fondness for fish

Gilbert White

There is a propensity belonging to common house cats that is very remarkable; I mean their violent fondness for fish, which appears to be their most favourite food. And yet nature in this instance seems to have planted in them an appetite that, unassisted, they know not how to gratify; for of all quadrupeds, cats are the least disposed towards water, and will not, when they can avoid it, deign to wet a foot, much less to plunge into that element.

From *Natural History of Selborne*
letter to Thomas Pennant Esq., 12 May 1770

The compleat angler

Charles Darwin

Mr Leonard, a very intelligent friend of mine, saw a cat catch a trout, by darting upon it in a deep clear water, at the mill at Weaford, near Lichfield. The cat belonged to Mr Stanley, who had often seen her catch fish in the same manner in summer, when the mill-pool was drawn so low that the fish could be seen. I have heard of other cats taking fish in shallow water, as they stood on the bank. This seems to be a natural method of taking their prey, usually lost by domestication, though they all retain a strong relish for fish.

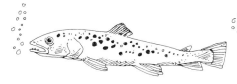

A Fondness for Fish

'... admorunt ubera tigres'

Gilbert White

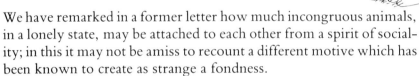

We have remarked in a former letter how much incongruous animals, in a lonely state, may be attached to each other from a spirit of sociality; in this it may not be amiss to recount a different motive which has been known to create as strange a fondness.

My friend had a little helpless leveret brought to him, which the servants fed with milk in a spoon, and about the same time his cat kittened, and the young were dispatched and buried. The hare was soon lost, and supposed to be gone the way of most foundlings, — to be killed by some dog or cat. However, in about a fortnight, as the master was sitting in his garden in the dusk of the evening, he observed his cat, with tail erect, trotting towards him, and calling with little short inward notes of complacency, such as they use towards their kittens, and something gambolling after, which proved to be the leveret that the cat had supported with her milk, and continued to support with great affection.

Thus was a graminivorous animal nurtured by a carnivorous and predaceous one!

Why so cruel and sanguinary a beast as a cat, of the ferocious genus of *Felis*, the *murium leo*, as Linnaeus calls it, should be affected with any tenderness towards an animal which is its natural prey, is not so easy to determine.

This strange affection probably was occasioned by that *desiderium*, those tender maternal feelings which the loss of her kittens had awakened in her breast; and by the complacency and ease she derived to herself from the procuring her teats to be drawn, which were too much distended with milk, till, from habit, she became as much delighted with this foundling as if it had been her real offspring.

This incident is no bad solution of that strange circumstance which grave historians as well as the poets assert, of exposed children being sometimes nurtured by female wild beasts that probably had lost their young. For it is not one whit more marvellous that Romulus and Remus, in their infant state, should be nursed by a she-wolf, than that a poor little sucking leveret should be fostered and cherished by a blood-thirsty grimalkin.

From *The Natural History and Antiquities of Selborne*
letter to the Hon. Daines Barrington, 9 May 1776

Nico the shepherd's cat

Sir Philip Sidney

I have (and long shall have) a white great nimble cat,
A king upon a mouse, a strong foe to the rat,
Fine eares, long taile he hath, with Lions curbed clawe,
Which oft he lifteth up, and stayes his lifted pawe,
Deepe musing to himselfe, which after-mewing showes,
Till with lickt beard, his eye of fire espie his foes.
      From Nico and Dorus, in the *Second Eclogues of Arcadia*

Cheetie-Poussie-Cattie, O

There was a wee bit mousikie,
That leeved in Gilberaty, O;
It couldna get a bit o cheese,
For Cheetie-Poussie-Cattie, O.

It said unto the cheesikie,
"O fain wad I be at ye, O,
If it werena for the cruel paws
O' Cheetie-Poussie-Cattie, O."

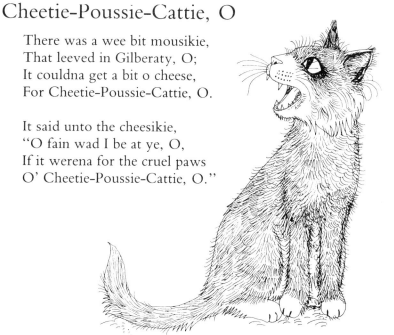

I Have a White Great Nimble Cat

On the death of a favourite cat drowned in a tub of gold-fishes

Thomas Gray

'Twas on a lofty vase's side.
Where China's gayest art had dyed
The azure flowers that blow,
Demurest of the tabby kind,
The pensive Selima, reclined,
Gazed on the lake below.

Her conscious tail her joy declared;
The fair round face, the snowy beard,
The velvet of her paws,
Her coat that with the tortoise vies,
Her ears of jet, and emerald eyes,
She saw, and purred applause.

Still had she gazed, but 'midst the tide,
Two angel forms were seen to glide—
The Genii of the stream:
Their scaly armour's Tyrian hue,
Through richest purple, to the view
Betrayed a golden gleam.

The hapless nymph with wonder saw:
A whisker first, and then a claw,
With many an ardent wish,
She stretched in vain to reach the prize:
What female heart can gold despise?
What cat's averse to fish?

Presumptuous maid! with looks intent,
Again she stretched, again she bent,
Nor knew the gulf between.
Malignant Fate sat by and smiled:
The slippery verge her feet beguiled;
She stumbled headlong in.

Eight times emerging from the flood,
She mewed to every watery god
Some speedy aid to send.
No Dolphin came, no Nereid stirred,
Nor cruel Tom or Susan heard;
A favourite has no friend!

From hence, ye Beauties! undeceived,
Know one false step is ne'er retrieved,
And be with caution bold:
Not all that tempts your wandering eyes
And heedless hearts is lawful prize,
Nor all that glisters, gold.

Last words to a dumb friend

Thomas Hardy

Pet was never mourned as you,
Purrer of the spotless hue,
Plumy tail and wistful gaze,
While you humoured our queer ways,
Or outshrilled your morning call
Up the stairs and through the hall—
Foot suspended in its fall—
While, expectant, you would stand
Arched, to meet the stroking hand;
Till your way you chose to wend
Yonder, to your tragic end.

Never another pet for me!
Let your place all vacant be;
Better blankness day by day
Than companion torn away.
Better bid his memory fade,
Better blot each mark he made,
Selfishly escape distress
By contrived forgetfulness,
Than preserve his prints to make
Every morn and eve an ache.

From the chair whereon he sat
Sweep his fur, nor wince thereat;
Rake his little pathways out
Mid the bushes round about;
Smooth away his talons' mark
From the claw-worn pine-tree bark,
Where he climbed as dusk enbrowned
Waiting us who loitered round.

Strange it is this speechless thing,
Subject to our mastering,
Subject for his life and food
To our gift, and time, and mood;
Timid pensioner of us Powers,
His existence ruled by ours,

Should—by crossing at a breath
Into safe and shielded death,
By the merely taking hence
Of his insignificance—
Loom as largened to the sense,
Shape as part, above man's will,
Of the Imperturbable.

As a prisoner, flight debarred,
Exercising in a yard,
Still retain I, troubled, shaken,
Mean estate, by him forsaken;
And this home, which scarcely took
Impress from his little look,
By his faring to the Dim,
Grows all eloquent of him.

Housemate, I can think you still
Bounding to the window-sill,
Over which I vaguely see
Your small mound beneath the tree,
Showing in the autumn shade
That you moulder where you played.

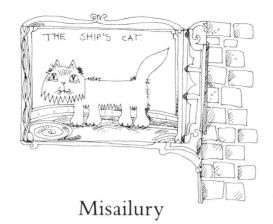

Misailury

'Some that are mad if they behold a cat' Shakespeare

From hence they passed to eels, then to parsnips, and then from one aversion to another, until we had worked ourselves up to such a pitch of complaisance, that when the dinner was to come in we enquired the name of every dish, and hoped that it would be of no offence to any of the company, before it was admitted. When we had sat down, this civility among us turned the discourse from eatables to other sorts of aversions; and the eternal cat, which plagues every conversation of this nature, began then to engross the subject. One had sweated at the sight of it, another had smelled it out as it lay concealed in a very distant cupboard; and he who crowned the whole set of these stories, reckoned up the number of times in which it had occasioned him to swoon away. 'At last,' sayd he, 'that you may all be satisfied of my invincible aversion to a cat, I shall give an unanswerable instance: As I was going through a street of London, where I never had been until then, I felt a general damp and faintness all over me, which I could not tell how to account for, until I chanced to cast my eyes upwards, and found that I was passing under a sign-post on which the picture of a cat was hung.'

From *The Spectator*, No. 538, 17 November 1712

The cats of the *Oceana*

Mark Twain

This *Oceana* is a stately big ship, luxuriously appointed ... cats—very friendly loafers; they wander all over the ship; the white one follows the chief steward around like a dog. There is also a basket of kittens. One of these cats goes ashore, in port, in England, Australia and India, to see how his various families are getting along, and is seen no more till the ship is ready to sail. No one knows how he finds out the sailing date, but no doubt he comes down to the dock every day and takes a look, and when he sees baggage and passengers flocking in, recognizes that it is time to get aboard. This is what the sailors believe. . . .

From *More Tramps Abroad*

Of all God's creatures

Mark Twain

Of all God's creatures there is only one that cannot be made the slave of the lash. That one is the cat. If man could be crossed with the cat it would improve man, but it would deteriorate the cat.

From *Notebook*

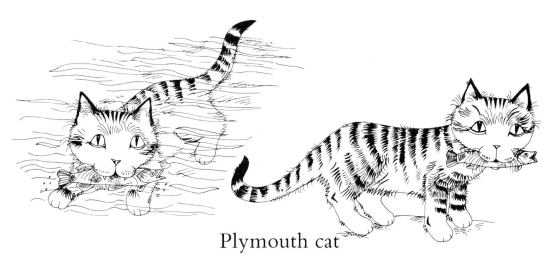

Plymouth cat

In the Battery at Devil's Point, one of the Plymouth defence works, there lives a cat who has a very clever way of catching fish. Fishing has become a habit with her and every day she plunges into the sea, catches a fish and carries it in her mouth into the Naval Guard-room, where she puts it down. The cat who is now seven years old has always been a good mouser and no doubt her experience in hunting water-rats has taught her to be bold and dive for fish, of which, as is well known, cats are particularly fond. Water has now become as necessary to her as to a Newfoundland dog and every day she goes along the rocky shore, ready at a moment's notice to plunge into the sea to grab her prey.

report in the *Plymouth Journal*, 1828

Raminagrobis, or the cat judge

La Fontaine

One day a lady weasel seized the home
Of a young rabbit who'd gone out to roam.
'Twas but a cunning trick the house to seize,
But master being out, a thing of ease.
So weasel brought her Household Gods to stay
What time our rabbit had just gone away
To pay his devoir to the rosy dawn
Amid the dew and thyme upon the lawn.
Now when he'd grazed and scampered here and there,
Back hurried Johnnie Rabbit to his lair.
"Ye Gods! What do I see? Am I quite sane?
Dame Weasel's nose pressed close against the pane!"
And loud he cried, "My father's house in pawn!

Here! Madam Weasel! Ere the trumpet sounds,
Evacuate my home; you're out of bounds;
Or else I'll call upon the regiment
Of rats, who all this countryside frequent".

Replied the lady of the pointed nose:
"To her who takes it first, possession falls;
Ah, what a *casus belli* for two foes,
A dwelling into which the owner crawls!
And even if it were a realm," said she,
"I'd really like to know what statute old
Has made the grant of properties freehold—
Perhaps to John, the son, descends the key.
Has Peter's nephew claims? or Will's? I'm told
They have more claim than Paul or even me!"

John Rabbit urged both custom and old use;
"These laws," said he, "this house gave me alone.
They made me master, me, my father's son;
To Peter first, then Simon, then me, John.
The first arrival! What a lame excuse!"
"Well, well," said Madam, "Say no more! To Puss,
Raminagrobis, then let's put our case."
This Cat a holy hermit's life enjoyed.

In truth demure, with holy life he toyed;
A holy man, he had a cat's own face,
Luxuriant fur and size and plumpy grace,
A skilful referee on any case.

To him as Judge, Jack Rabbit did agree
And there and then each claimant made a plea
Before His Royal Furry Majesty.
The Cat whom some call Grippeminaud, with glee
Remarked: "Approach, my dears, this deaf old cat."
Without alarm they came towards his mat.
When Grippeminaud, the sanctimonious knave,
Saw them within his reach, he bared his claws;
He seized his prey whom wisdom could not save
And made the two agree within his jaws.

From *Fables*

Parson Woodforde's stiony

The Rev. James Woodforde

The Stiony on my right Eye-lid still swelled and inflamed very much. As it is commonly said that the Eye-lid being rubbed by the tail of a black Cat would do it much good if not entirely cure it, and having a black Cat, a little before dinner I made a trial of it, and very soon after dinner I found my Eye-lid much abated of the swelling and almost free from Pain. I cannot therefore but conclude it to be of the greatest service to a Stiony on the Eye-lid. Any other Cat's Tail may have the above effect in all probability—but I did my Eye-lid with my own black Tom Cat's Tail.

(Stiony, more usually Styany, is a contraction of 'Sty-on-eye')

Puss passer-by

Edmund Gosse

Puss passer-by, within this simple tomb
Lies one whose life fell Atropos hath shred;
The happiest cat on earth hath heard her doom,
And sleeps for ever in a marble bed.
Alas! what long delicious days I've seen!
O cats of Egypt, my illustrious sires,
You who on altars, bound with garlands green,
Have melted hearts, and kindled fond desires;
Hymns in your praise were paid, and offerings too,
But I'm not jealous of those rites divine,
Since Ludovisa loved me, close and true,
Your ancient glory was less proud than mine.
To live, a simply pussy, by her side
Was nobler far than to be deified.

> tr. from La Mothe le Vayer on the
> favourite cat of the Duchess of Maine

Epitaph

Worn out with age and dire disease, a cat,
Friendly to all save wicked mouse and rat,
I'm sent at last to ford the Stygian lake,
And to the infernal coast a voyage make.
Me Proserpine received, and smiling said:
"Be blessed within these mansions of the dead.
Enjoy among thy velvet-footed loves,
Elysium's sunny banks, and shady groves!"
"But if I've well deserved (O gracious Queen),
If patient under sufferings I have been,
Grant me at least one night to visit home again,
Once more to see my home and mistress dear,
And purr these grateful accents in her ear:
'Thy faithful cat, thy poor departed slave,
Still loves her mistress, e'en beyond the grave.'"

translated by Dr Jortin

Index